ACCESS
READING
TEST

Forms A &

MANUAL

Colin McCarty and Mary Crumpler

Hodder Murray
A MEMBER OF THE HODDER HEADLINE GROUP

Acknowledgements

We thank Margaret Lorman-Hall and her team for marking all the answer booklets from the standardisation trials and entering the data. This ensured the highest quality of marking and reliability for the independent statistical analyses and reports prepared by Tony Kiek.

We also are much indebted to Marie Lallaway, Jenny Vaughan and Mike de la Mare as key members of the team authoring the reading pieces and generating the questions.

We are profoundly grateful to our publisher, Charles Knight, for his close involvement and encouragement throughout all stages of this project and his many helpful suggestions and advice.

We wish to record our thanks to the staff and students in the following schools, organisations and services, who took part in the standardisation trials:

All Saints Primary School, Coventry
Allesley Primary School, Coventry
Aylesbury Training Group, Aylesbury
BETA, Basingstoke
Brenda Soar Training, Newmarket
Brinsworth Training Ltd, Rotherham
Chesham High School, Chesham
Coventry Learning Support Service
Dr Challoner's Grammar School, High Wycombe
Fort Hill School, Basingstoke
Grange Farm Primary School, Coventry
Gryphon School, Sherborne
Haresfoot Preparatory School, Cheshunt
HETA, Humberside
John Gulson Primary School, Coventry

Kingham Hill School, Kingham Hill
Leamington Centre, Warwickshire College
Limbrick Wood Primary School, Coventry
Little Heath School, Tilehurst
Mountfitchet High School, Stansted
Queens' School, Bushey
Sarah Craig, Dyslexia Tutor, Folkestone
St Bernadette's Primary School, Wallsend
Swanbourne House School, Milton Keynes
The Hurst Community College, Tadley
Twynham School, Christchurch
Westbourne House School, Chichester
Whitely Abbey Primary School, Coventry
Windsor and Maidenhead Learning Support Service

Orders: please contact Bookpoint Ltd, 130 Milton Park, Abingdon, Oxon OX14 4SB. Telephone: (44) 01235 827720. Fax: (44) 01235 400454. Lines are open from 9.00 to 5.00, Monday to Saturday, with a 24 hour message answering service. You can also order through our website www.hodderheadline.co.uk.

British Library Cataloguing in Publication Data
A catalogue record for this title is available from the British Library

ISBN-10 0 340 91283 9
ISBN-13 978 0 340 91283 6

First published 2006

Impression number   10 9 8 7 6 5 4 3 2 1
Year   2010 2009 2008 2007 2006

Copyright © 2006 Hodder and Stoughton Ltd

Typeset by Fakenham Photosetting Limited, Fakenham, Norfolk.
Printed in Great Britain for Hodder Murray, a division of Hodder Headline, 338 Euston Road, London NW1 3BH, by Hobbs the Printers Ltd, Totton, Hampshire SO40 3WX.

Contents

1 Introduction

The **Access Reading Test** is designed for use across the 7 to 20+ age range. It comprises two parallel forms (Form A and Form B), created to provide matched reading experiences.

Each Form contains 60 questions and is based on eleven varied pieces of reading material: the table below indicates the different styles of question and the four key reading skills that are being assessed. These represent distinct subtests: the scoring grid on the front cover of each test booklet has been designed to allow you to subtotal each of these reading skills for diagnostic purposes.

Reading skill	Question style	Number of items
Literal comprehension	These require students to obtain information directly from instructions and factual records.	20
Vocabulary	These ask students to choose alternative words which are closest in meaning to given words.	15
Comprehension requiring inference or prediction and opinions	Here the items require matching opinions to 'talking heads' or matching a quotation to an inference.	16
Comprehension requiring analysis	These questions use an agree/disagree/does not say style of answering to check if students understand meaning within a passage.	9

The tests are also designed to provide material at three broad levels of experience: primary, early secondary and later secondary into adulthood. This is detailed below, where the finer breakdown reflects the increasing experience needed to be able to read different types of material with understanding – often called the *level of demand*.

Section in test	Age-appropriateness	Key Stage of source material	Number of questions in section	Topic or information about question styles
Literal comprehension				
1	7–11	KS2	8	advertisements
6	11–13	KS3	7	brochures
9	14–20+	KS4	5	reports
Vocabulary				
2	7–11	KS2	5	selecting from four choices the word which most closely matches the meaning of a target word
5	11–13	KS3	5	
11	14–20+	KS4	5	
Inference				
3	7–11	KS2	4	talking heads
8	11–13	KS3	6	quotes and reasons
10	14–20+	KS4	6	talking heads
Analysis				
4	7–11	KS2	4	agree, disagree, does not say
7	11–13	KS3	5	agree, disagree, does not say

Purposes and uses of the test

The *Access Reading Test* provides a standardised assessment of a pupil's/student's reading attainment. It enables you to explore the types of reading skill that he or she is able to use effectively to extract meaning from a text and those which may need further teaching and practice. It is quick to administer – the standard time allowed for the test is 30 minutes – and straightforward to mark, as the questions are all in 'objective' formats.

For each pupil/student, the test gives three 'global' measures of reading attainment:

- standardised score;
- reading age;
- percentile.

For those teachers and tutors wanting a more detailed picture, the test also gives valuable information about:

- the performance of pupils and students on each question – the *facility*, or proportion that answered correctly – for each year group, so that comparisons may easily be made.

- average scores – by chronological age cohort and year group – in each of the four reading skills assessed:

  - literal comprehension;
  - understanding of vocabulary;
  - comprehension requiring inference or prediction and opinions;
  - comprehension requiring analysis.

The look-up tables in this manual allow you to make quite detailed comparisons of individual patterns of performance against the norms and patterns for the age or year. In this way, it is hoped that the information will help teachers to make better informed judgements when developing individual action plans with pupils or individual education plans (IEPs) and intervention programmes, or when completing Assessment Focuses on reading ability.

It is also possible to use the test to determine if extra time allows a slower-reading pupil significantly to improve their score. Evidence of this nature may be used to support an application for extra time in national tests such as those at Key Stages 2 and 3 or GCSE.

The *Access Reading Test* comes in two parallel forms, A and B, so that shorter-term progress may be monitored and measured. Where there is a longer interval, such as a year or more, between each administration, and the parallel form has already been used, it is permissible to re-test using the same form.

The *Access Reading Test* may also be used as a group baseline test to determine which pupils may benefit from further, individual assessment.

2 Administering the Test

Giving the test

Group size

The test is designed to enable it to be administered to whole classes or large groups, but it may be used with individuals or small groups if this is preferred.

Which form to use?

Forms A and B are highly reliable alternate forms, which are matched in content and difficulty, so either can be used if the pupils/students have not previously taken the test. If they have, you should always use the alternate form. It is advisable to wait at least a year if re-testing a pupil/student who has already been assessed on both forms.

Timing

A time limit of **30 minutes** is set for the test. In practice, it is likely to take less than 25 minutes for most classes, unless they are very slow readers.

Preparation

Each pupil/student will need either Form A or Form B of the test booklet, and writing materials. Answers may be altered by rubbing or crossing out.

Test conditions

It is important that the pupils/students work alone, without copying or discussing their answers.

Administration

Give each pupil/student a copy of the booklet. Ask them to complete the details on the front cover – their first name and their surname, their gender, date of birth and the date of testing. There are spaces also for the name of their school/college and class/group.

- Introduce the test by telling them that they will be reading a number of texts and answering questions about them.
- They should do their best to try to answer all the questions by ticking a letter or joining dots to letters.
- They should choose their best guess if they are not sure of an answer, unless you deliberately wish pupils/students to omit questions that they find too difficult, to inform an *Assessment for Learning Strategy*. (Scores are likely to be slightly depressed if guessing is actively discouraged.)
- Tell them that there will be some sections that they can do easily, but that there are also some harder sections and the test generally gets harder towards the end.
- They should not worry if they find some questions difficult, but just try their best.

If any of the pupils/students are not clear about what they have to do, you may give additional explanation to help them to understand the requirements of the test, but do not read any of the questions or answer choices to them, nor help them with individual words.

Marking the test and recording scores

Once the pupil has completed the *Access Reading Test* their answers may be marked and, if required, analysed. Mark each question as correct or incorrect, awarding one mark for each correct answer, as given below: for the resulting scores to be valid, you should not deviate from this mark scheme or award half-marks.

A short line is available in the right-hand margin of the test booklets for you to tick so that each section may be easily added up. To assist marking and collating the data, there are boxes in which to record section totals at the bottom right of each appropriate page of the test booklets.

Transfer the raw scores from the bottom of each section to the 'raw score' column of the scoring grid on the front cover of the test and calculate the total raw score. The totals for each 'reading skill' can then be found by using the subtest scores column on the right of the summary box. These can then be used with the diagnostic information in Tables 1–5 to help you decide what areas of strengths and weaknesses need to be addressed with the pupil/student.

Evaluating the evidence for extra time

Do not let any student/pupil spend longer than 30 minutes working on the test unless you are making an 'extra time' assessment to support an application for extra time in national tests or public examinations.

Pupils/students who have not completed the test in 30 minutes may then be given 25% extra time – i.e. 7½ minutes – if you feel this is appropriate and you wish to see if there is an improvement in their score with the extra time. They should mark on the paper where they reached after 30 minutes by writing '30 mins' against the question number, and change to a different coloured pen.

They can then use the extra time to complete the test and/or go back and review (and change, if they wish) earlier answers. All must stop after 37½ minutes. It is important that pupils complete the test in a *single* session.

The two scores – in the standard time and with extra time – can then be directly compared to establish whether they meet the performance criteria prescribed by the examining body.

Answers

Question	Form A	Form B	Question	Form A	Form B
1	D	C	31	A	A
2	C	B	32	B	B
3	B	A	33	A	A
4	C	B	34	B	A
5	D	B	35	C	C
6	C	B	36	A	C
7	B	C	37	B	A
8	B	A	38	A	B
9	B	B	39	B	B
10	A	C	40	D	A
11	D	C	41	C	G
12	B	D	42	E	D
13	B	B	43	F	C
14	A	A	44	H	E
15	C	B	45	A	A
16	B	C	46	D	A
17	E	E	47	A	B
18	B	B	48	A	A
19	C	B	49	D	C
20	A	A	50	A	E
21	C	C	51	C	C
22	C	C	52	B	B
23	C	A	53	D	C
24	C	C	54	C	A
25	B	D	55	E	D
26	B	B	56	C	A
27	C	A	57	C	C
28	B	B	58	D	B
29	C	C	59	D	A
30	B	C	60	A	C

3 Obtaining and Interpreting Test Scores

Each young person is an individual with a mix of strengths and weaknesses across all that they do. Every pupil/student may be expected to show a different pattern of strengths and weakness when reading. The **Access Reading Test** enables you to swiftly check his or her performance in a variety of ways.

Obtaining standardised scores

The pupil's chronological age on taking the test should first be calculated in years and completed months. The standardised score may then be found from Table A, at the end of this manual. Reading ages and percentile scores are given in Tables 1 and 2 below.

Where pupils/students have not done well, we suggest their answers are first analysed – as described below – to identify any specific patterns of weakness. An oral reading test, such as the **Diagnostic Reading Analysis**, by Crumpler and McCarty, may be a next step to explore strengths and weaknesses and determine strategies to improve their reading skills.

How to use the information

1 **You will be able to check against national norms** using:
   - standardised scores (Table A);
   - reading ages (Table 1);
   - percentiles (Table 2);
   - average scores for each age range, by gender and NC level (Table 3).

These standardised results are valuable, but only give an *overall* picture of the young person relative to his/her peers. Such data may, for example, confirm that the student is doing well for his/her age and indicate that no intervention strategy is required. However, a more detailed check may show that a very strong performance in one aspect of reading – for example, literal comprehension – is masking a weakness in, say, analysis, and thereby inform the completion of Assessment Focuses (AFs) for Assessing Pupil Performance. This manual explains how to mine down into the data to gather more useful information.

2 **You may inspect the numbers of correct answers to see if there are patterns of strengths and weakness** in:
   - Literal comprehension (*AF1, AF2*);
   - Vocabulary (*AF1*);
   - Inference (*AF3, AF6*);
   - Analysis (*AF3, AF6*).

The scoring grid on the front of the test booklet enables you to collate this information, and you may then review the student's performance by comparison to an age group or a school year group (Tables 4 and 5 respectively). If performance is similar in each of the categories, then the student will be unusual – most students find literal comprehension and vocabulary easier than comprehension requiring inference, prediction or analysis.

A quick glance at Tables 4 and 5 shows the typical patterns for the number of questions correct. For example, for Year 10 students:

	Literal	Vocabulary	Inference	Analysis
	15	12	11	6
Expressed as percentages:	75%	80%	69%	67%

A closer inspection shows that this pattern holds fairly true across all years.

The two case studies (see pages 18–20) indicate how this comparative information enables some next steps to be planned. With this more detailed picture, it is possible to design specific teaching strategies to help weak, modest and even good readers to improve.

3 You may also go one stage further and check a student's individual performance on a specific question or group of questions and compare how they have performed relative to other students in the same year group.

Refer to Table B (at the end of this manual), for the test form used, to see what proportion of students in that year group answered the question correctly. This is called the *facility* and is shown as a decimal: a facility value of 0.6 means 60% answered the question correctly. It also helps you to find which questions students, on average, found difficult and how performance improves with age and experience.

Reading ages

Reading age is used by many teachers as a quick reference: a reading age shows the *average* chronological age of the students who obtained each particular raw score – i.e. the chronological age at which this level of performance is typical. For more detailed comparative information, however, standardised scores and percentiles are to be preferred.

Note that **ART** reading ages below 7:0 are statistical extrapolations, because the **Access Reading Test** is not designed for children below 7:0, and therefore was not standardised on younger age groups. Such extrapolations can nevertheless be useful in interpreting the performance of older, less able pupils.

Table 1: Reading ages (Forms A & B)

Raw Score	Reading Age	Raw Score	Reading Age
1–13	below 5:6	36	12:3
14	5:6	37	12:9
15	5:9	38	13:0
16	6:2	39	13:3
17	6:5	40	13:9
18	6:7	41	14:0
19	6:10	42	14:6
20	7:0	43	14:9
21	7:2	44	15:0
22	7:6	45	15:6
23	710	46	15:9
24	8:2	47	16:3
25	8:6	48	16:6
26	8:10	49	16:9
27	9:3	50	17:3
28	9:7	51	17:6
29	9:11	52	17:9
30	10:3	53	18:3
31	10:7	54	18:6
32	10:11	55	19:0
33	11:4	56	19:3
34	11:8	57	19:6
35	12:0	58–60	20:0+

Standardised scores and percentiles

The Technical Information reported in this manual (page 21) indicates that the performance data provided by the *Access Reading Test* is both robust and reliable. However, reading age norms do not adequately convey the *significance* of scores above or below the average or median. For example, if a child scores a reading age one year above, or two years below, his or her chronological age, it is not clear *how* superior or inferior these scores actually are.

To assist teachers to gain a better feel for the significance of a pupil's reading age, percentiles are more useful, because they show the percentage

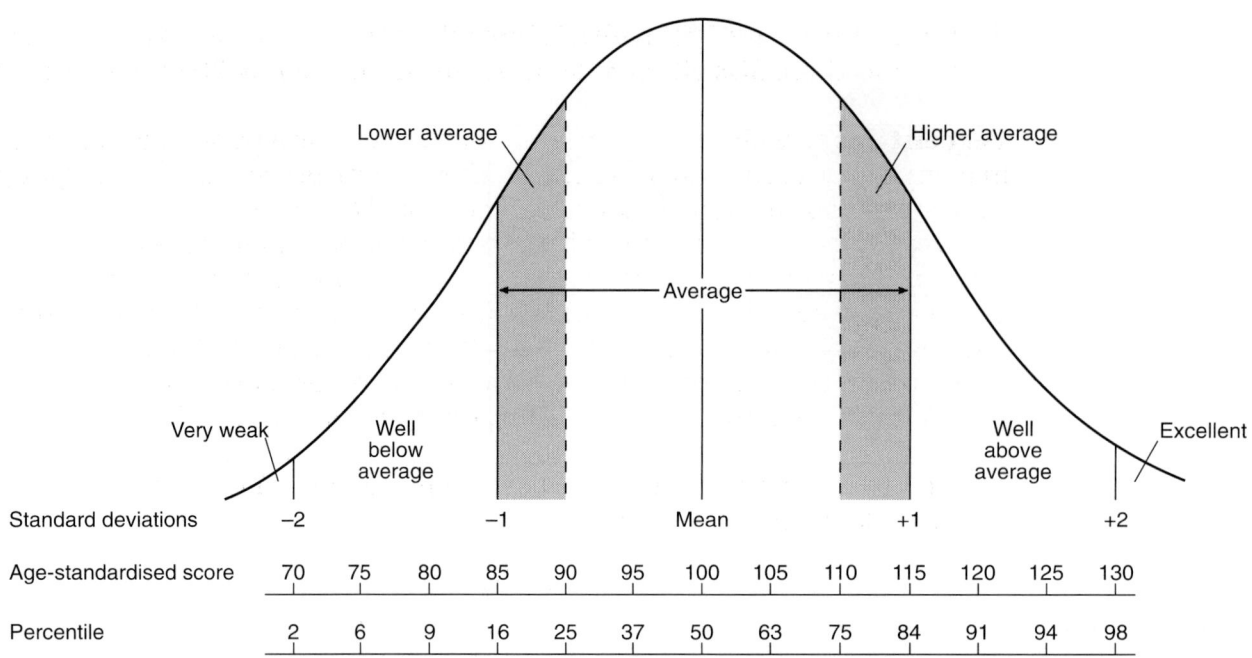

Standardised score	Qualitative interpretation of standardised scores	Standard deviation from mean	Percentile score	Percentage of normal population
>130	Excellent	>+2	>98	2.27
116–130	Well above average	+1 to +2	84–98	13.59
110–115 85–115 *85–90*	*higher average* Average/age-appropriate *lower average*	−1 to +1	16–83	68.26
70–84	Well below average	−1 to −2	2–15	13.59
<69	Very weak	<−2	<2	2.27

Figure 1: Relationship between standardised test scores and qualitative interpretations

in each age group who score above a certain level. For example, a pupil aged 11:0 with a raw score of 39 falls at the 80th percentile (and has a standardised score of 113), meaning that this score is reached or exceeded only by the top 20 per cent of that age group. This raw score, though, is only two marks of raw score above the average for all 11 year olds, yet corresponds to a reading age of 13:3. In other words, a small change in raw score may well have a disproportionate effect on the information, and this should always be borne in mind.

The relationship between standardised scores and percentiles is most easily seen by reference to Figure 1.

The **standardised scores** provided by Table A range between 70 and 130, and the mean is 100. The five bands determined by the standard deviation (SD) of 15, enable you to group pupils into:

- those whose performance is within an age-appropriate range (within one SD either side of the mean: i.e. 85–115);
- those who are below or above average in this regard (between one and two SDs either side of the mean: i.e. 70–85 and 115–130);

- those who are *well* below/*well* above the average for their age (between two and three SDs either side of the mean: i.e. below 70 or above 130).

Percentiles give alternative information concerning a pupil's performance in comparison to his or her age group. They show the *percentage* of the group from whom norms were obtained, which scored *below* the pupil's standardised score. So a standardised score at the 68th percentile is comfortably within the average range, since it means that 68 per cent of the group scored below the pupil's standardised score. A standardised score at the 16th percentile, however, means that only 16 per cent had a lower result. Scores below the 16th percentile (i.e. two standard deviations below the mean) are of concern, as they indicate performance that is well below average.

To get a pupil's percentile score, first obtain his/her standardised score (from Table A), then refer to Table 2.

Table 2: Percentiles

Standardised score	Percentile	Standardised score	Percentile	Standardised score	Percentile
139+	99+	109	72	89	24
133–8	99	108	70	88	22
130–2	98	107	68	87	20
128–9	97	106	66	86	18
126–7	96	105	63	85	16
125	95	104	60	84	14
123–4	94	103	58	83	13
122	93	102	55	82	12
121	92	101	52	81	11
120	91	100	50	80	9
119	90	99	48	79	8
118	89	98	45	78	7
117	87	97	42	76–7	6
116	86	96	40	75	5
115	84	95	37	73–4	4
114	82	94	34	71–2	3
113	80	93	32	70	2
112	78	92	30	70–	1
111	77	91	28		
110	74	90	26		

Relating test scores to National Curriculum levels

Table 3 gives, at a quick glance, the average raw scores attained by males and females in different age cohorts. To allow teachers to make a comparison to National Curriculum performance, the mean or average National Curriculum level for each cohort is also provided. For ages 7 through to 11, the average key stage level was derived from either pupils' KS1 English level or information obtained from the QCA 'Optional Tests' for the appropriate year. For ages 11 to 14, the level obtained was the KS2 English level or again from the 'Optional Test' information. From 14 to 16, it is the level obtained from KS3 English National Curriculum results. The results from 16:0 onwards are based on GCSE grades, where a C is equivalent to NC level 7 and B equivalent to NC level 8.

The data for this comparison was supplied by teachers in many, but not all, schools in the trials, so it is less robust than the data used for the standardised scores and all other tables. The National Curriculum levels shown in bold are those obtained directly from a key stage result; those not in bold are obtained from Optional Tests.

Table 3: Average *ART* raw scores by gender, age and NC level

Age	Form A			Form B			Average NC English Level
	Males	*Females*	*Total*	*Males*	*Females*	*Total*	
7:0–7:11	15.17	13.97	14.59	15.62	14.76	15.21	**2.4**
8:0–8:11	19.07	19.97	19.49	20.15	21.18	20.63	2.8
9:0–9:11	25.66	25.75	25.70	25.32	26.46	25.84	3.6
10:0–10:11	31.09	31.69	31.39	31.13	32.38	31.75	4.0
11:0–11:11	37.32	38.08	37.68	36.63	37.40	37.00	**4.4**
12:0–12:11	38.77	40.46	39.56	37.66	40.10	38.80	4.3
13:0–13:11	40.02	42.92	41.44	38.12	40.95	39.51	4.1
14:0–14:11	43.58	45.53	44.53	41.32	44.50	42.86	**5.1**
15:0–15:11	45.38	46.25	45.78	42.80	44.37	43.53	5.3
16:0–16:11	49.08	50.00	49.43	46.80	48.27	47.36	**7.1 (= C)**
17:0–17:11	49.87	52.30	50.74	48.08	50.66	49.01	8.0 (= B)
18:0–18:11	50.79	53.55	51.56	47.79	49.82	48.36	7.9 (= B)
19:0–19:11	49.31	51.00	49.43	48.46	48.00	48.43	–
20:0–24:11	48.91	53.00	49.25	48.91	51.00	49.08	–

As these average levels for each cohort have been supplied by teachers translating information from – in most cases – National Curriculum Optional Tests, they must be considered to be indicative of the average level of the cohort.

Comparing performance in the different subtests

Tables 4 and 5 provide information as to how each age cohort has scored in each of the four subtests. By using Table 4, you can review or compare each pupil's performance against the ages in the standardisation cohorts to see if a pupil shows any significant strengths or weaknesses against the patterns illustrated.

As the genres and vocabulary used in the test were guided by the English *National Literacy Strategy* and the *Framework for Teaching English: Years 7, 8 and 9*, Table 5 presents average scores for each Year group. The tables are presented as both ages and years to facilitate teachers who may record data either by chronological age or by year group.

If there is concern about answers to a specific question, say, then reference to the facilities in Table B (see page 30) will allow you to compare the pupil's or class's performance to that of the Year cohorts in the standardisation trials. The information in these tables may be helpful in providing comparative evidence to assist in completing Assessment Focuses (*AF*s) in Assessing Pupil Performance documentation.

For ease of reference, the breakdown of the subtests is repeated here (the second table on page 4 contains more detailed information about the level of the questions in each subtest).

Reading skill	Question style	Number of items
Literal comprehension	These require students to obtain information directly from instructions and factual records.	20
Vocabulary	These ask students to choose alternative words which are closest in meaning to given words.	15
Comprehension requiring inference or prediction and opinions	Here the items require matching opinions to 'talking heads' or matching a quotation to an inference.	16
Comprehension requiring analysis	These questions use an agree/disagree/does not say style of answering to check if students understand meaning within a passage.	9

Table 4: Average scores by subtest, gender and age

Age	Literal (max 20)			Vocabulary (max 15)			Inference (max 16)			Analysis (max 9)		
	Males	*Females*	*Total*	*Males*	*Females*	*Total*	*Males*	*Females*	*Total*	*Males*	*Females*	*Total*
7:0–7:11	6.6	6.4	6.5	4.0	3.9	3.9	2.4	1.9	2.1	2.4	2.2	2.3
8:0–8:11	8.0	8.5	8.2	5.3	5.3	5.3	3.3	3.5	3.4	3.0	3.4	3.2
9:0–9:11	9.7	10.3	9.9	6.8	6.7	6.8	5.3	5.1	5.2	3.8	4.1	3.9
10:0–10:11	11.1	11.7	11.4	8.7	8.4	8.5	6.9	7.3	7.1	4.4	4.7	4.6
11:0–11:11	13.1	13.3	13.2	10.2	10.4	10.3	8.5	8.8	8.7	5.1	5.2	5.2
12:0–12:11	13.6	14.0	13.8	10.6	11.1	10.8	8.8	9.7	9.2	5.3	5.5	5.4
13:0–13:11	13.9	14.6	14.3	10.9	11.5	11.2	9.0	10.4	9.7	5.3	5.5	5.4
14:0–14:11	14.8	15.6	15.2	11.8	12.2	12.0	10.4	11.3	10.8	5.6	6.0	5.8
15:0–15:11	15.4	15.6	15.5	12.0	12.3	12.1	10.9	11.5	11.2	5.8	5.9	5.9
16:0–16:11	16.4	16.5	16.4	12.9	13.1	13.0	12.5	13.2	12.7	6.2	6.3	6.3
17:0–17:11	16.6	17.5	16.9	13.1	13.4	13.2	12.8	14.1	13.3	6.5	6.5	6.5
18:0–18:11	17.0	17.2	17.1	13.3	13.4	13.3	12.7	14.1	13.1	6.3	7.0	6.5
19:0–19:11	16.9	17.0	16.9	12.9	14.0	13.0	13.4	13.5	13.4	5.7	5.0	5.7
20:0–24:11	16.9	18.5	17.0	13.2	14.0	13.3	12.5	13.5	12.6	6.3	6.0	6.3

Table 5: Average scores by subtest, gender and Year group in England

Year	Literal (max 20)			Vocabulary (max 15)			Inference (max 16)			Analysis (max 9)		
	Males	Females	Total	Males	Females	Total	Males	Females	Total	Males	Females	Total
3	6.6	6.6	6.6	4.1	3.9	4.0	2.2	2.0	2.1	2.4	2.3	2.4
4	8.5	9.1	8.8	5.7	5.4	5.7	3.8	4.2	4.0	3.3	3.6	3.4
5	10.0	10.6	10.3	7.1	7.1	7.1	5.6	5.4	5.5	3.9	4.2	4.1
6	11.6	12.2	11.9	9.3	8.9	9.1	7.5	7.9	7.7	4.5	4.8	4.7
7	13.3	13.5	13.4	10.4	10.6	10.5	8.6	9.0	8.8	5.2	5.3	5.3
8	13.6	14.1	13.8	10.6	11.1	10.8	8.7	9.8	9.2	5.2	5.4	5.3
9	14.2	15.1	14.6	11.1	11.9	11.5	9.3	11.0	10.1	5.3	5.7	5.5
10	15.0	15.5	15.3	11.9	12.0	12.0	10.7	11.3	11.0	5.7	6.0	5.8
11	15.2	15.7	15.4	12.0	12.5	12.2	10.8	11.9	11.3	5.7	6.0	5.8
12	17.1	17.4	17.2	13.4	13.5	13.4	13.3	13.9	13.5	6.6	6.5	6.5
13	16.9	17.4	17.1	13.4	13.4	13.4	13.0	14.2	13.5	6.5	6.6	6.5
FE trainees	16.5	17.0	16.5	12.8	12.2	12.8	12.5	12.3	12.5	6.2	5.5	6.2

Two case studies

Holly

Holly took Form B of the *Access Reading Test* on 23 November 2005. Her date of birth is 17 May 1994, so she was 11 years 6 months old at the time of testing. Her scores for the different sections of the test were:

Section		Raw score	Subtest scores			
Section 1	Literal comprehension	6	**Literal comprehension**			
Section 2	Vocabulary	4	Sections 1 + 6 + 9 =	10		
Section 3	Inference	4	**Vocabulary**			
Section 4	Analysis	3	Sections 2 + 5 + 11 =	11		
Section 5	Vocabulary	4	**Inference**			
Section 6	Literal comprehension	3	Sections 3 + 8 + 10 =	9		
Section 7	Analysis	2	**Analysis**			
Section 8	Inference	3	Sections 4 + 7 =	5		
Section 9	Literal comprehension	1				
Section 10	Inference	2				
Section 11	Vocabulary	3	**Chronological age** 11:6		**Reading age** 12:0	
Total raw score		35	**Standardised score** 103		**Percentile** 58	

Firstly, Holly's teacher referred to the Age Standardisation table (Table A) to find Holly's standardised score and the Reading Ages table (Table 1) and entered the results on the test booklet: they were 103 and 12:0 years respectively.

Then Holly's teacher compared Holly's overall raw score of 35 with the results of other girls in the 11:0–11:11 age range, as given in Table 3, and found that the average raw score was 37.

Her teacher then calculated Holly's four subtest scores, and compared these with those of other girls of her age, using Table 4.

Subtest	Holly's scores	Average score for girls aged 11:0–11:11
Literal comprehension	10	13
Vocabulary	11	10
Inference	9	9
Analysis	5	5

From this, it can be seen that Holly has a relative weakness with literal comprehension as compared with her peers, although she is able to draw inferences from texts and analyse underlying ideas at the average level for her age. This suggests that Holly skimmed the passages for the general, underlying ideas without focusing on every detail and/or answered the questions from memory without referring back to the text to confirm that her choices were correct.

Daniel

Daniel also took Form B of the **Access Reading Test** on 23 November 2005. His date of birth is 1 July 1995, so at the time of testing he was 10 years 4 months old. His scores for the different sections of the test were:

Section		Raw score	Subtest scores		
Section 1	Literal comprehension	7	**Literal comprehension**		
Section 2	Vocabulary	5	Sections 1 + 6 + 9 = 12		
Section 3	Inference	4	**Vocabulary**		
Section 4	Analysis	2	Sections 2 + 5 + 11 = 13		
Section 5	Vocabulary	4	**Inference**		
Section 6	Literal comprehension	2	Sections 3 + 8 + 10 = 15		
Section 7	Analysis	4	**Analysis**		
Section 8	Inference	6	Sections 4 + 7 = 6		
Section 9	Literal comprehension	3			
Section 10	Inference	5			
Section 11	Vocabulary	4	**Chronological age** 10:4	**Reading age**	15:9
Total raw score		46	**Standardised score** >128	**Percentile**	>97

Firstly, Daniel's teacher referred to the Age Standardisation table (Table A) to find Daniel's standardised score and the Reading Ages table (Table 1) and entered the results on the test booklet: they were >128 and 15:9 respectively. (Standardised scores for raw scores above 44 could not be calculated for pupils of 10 years 4 months, as this is well above age-expectations.)

Daniel's teacher then compared his overall raw score of 46 with the results of other boys in the 10:0–10:11 age range as given in Table 3, and found that the average was 31. Daniel's score, therefore, was significantly higher than that of his peers.

His teacher then calculated Daniel's four subtest scores, and compared these with those of other boys of his age, using Table 4.

Subtest	Daniel's scores	Average score for boys aged 10:00–10:11
Literal comprehension	12	11
Vocabulary	13	9
Inference	15	7
Analysis	6	4

From this, it can be seen that Daniel's literal comprehension of texts is broadly comparable with those of other boys of his age. However, his vocabulary and ability to analyse and draw inferences from what he has read are more advanced than those of his peers. Looking further down the age bands in Table 4, his teacher could see that Daniel's vocabulary score is comparable to that of males in the 16:00–16:11 age range; his ability to analyse texts is comparable to males in the 15:00–16:11 age range, and his raw score for the subtest measuring the ability to drawing inferences exceeded the mean raw score for any of the age groups tested.

In relative terms, Daniel – although a far better reader than Holly – may still be weak at 'test-taking techniques', as the answers for literal comprehension are clearly presented in the text. It may be that before re-testing using the parallel form, both pupils would benefit from a discussion about how to engage with pencil-and-paper tests and be encouraged to develop their skills of information handling and retrieval.

4 Technical Information

Trialling and standardisation

Prior to the standardisation, the authors worked with teachers in Hyde Park Junior School and Kingham Hill School trialling the draft papers. This information, together with meetings with members of the Learning Support team of Coventry LEA, who gave much valuable advice, allowed us to refine a number of pieces of text, revise some of the artwork, and select and improve a number of questions from those originally drafted.

Between September and December 2005, over 4000 school pupils, students and trainees took part in the standardisation trials for Forms A and B: the schools and organisations involved are listed in the acknowledgements at the front of the manual. Table 6 gives the numbers of pupils/students at each age that formed the final marked standardisation sample, and indicates that the standardisation is robust in terms of numbers.

Table 6: The numbers in each age cohort in the standardisation sample

Age (years:months)	Number of males	Number of females	Total numbers
7:0–7:11	108	101	209
8:0–8:11	167	146	313
9:0–9:11	150	123	273
10:0–10:11	113	110	223
11:0–11:11	411	373	784
12:0–12:11	341	300	641
13:0–13:11	240	230	470
14:0–14:11	212	199	411
15:0–15:11	183	158	341
16:0–16:11	127	79	206
17:0–17:11	100	56	156
18:0–18:11	28	11	39
19:0–19:11	13	1	14
20:0–24:11	11	1	12
Total	**2204**	**1888**	**4092**

The age-standardisation process

Age-standardised test scores take into account a pupil's age, so that we have an indication of how each pupil is performing relative to other pupils of the same age. The objective of the age-standardisation process is to produce a look-up table with columns classified across the top by age (in years and completed months) and rows by test raw score. Each cell of the table contains a *standardised score* value which represents the raw score adjusted for the pupil's age.

To enable age-standardisation of a particular test, a 'one-off' standardisation trial is held, involving a large sample of pupils who must be representative of the backgrounds, abilities and age ranges of the population for whom the 'live' test is intended.

The convention in educational assessment is that the mean or average standardised score for each age group is 100 with a standard deviation of 15. This means that if a pupil achieves a standardised score of 100, then that pupil has average ability for their age. About two-thirds of pupils will have standardised scores between 85 and 115. About 16% of pupils will score above 115, and the remaining 16% will score below 85 (see Figure 1, on page 12).

Reliability

The *reliability* of a test indicates whether or not we would get similar results from repeated administrations of the test with similar samples of pupils and students. An appropriate measure of test reliability for this test is Cronbach's Alpha (α), which measures internal consistency reliability. A value above 0.60 is considered acceptable for most forms of educational assessment.

Test theory tells us that test reliability is also related to test length, and suggests that any test should comprise at least 30 items to achieve reasonable reliability. In fact the **Access Reading Test** Forms A and B each comprise 60 items, so we can expect their test reliabilities to be very high. The α values for Form A and B are both excellent, at 0.95 and 0.94 respectively, and provide highly reliable measures of reading.

Validity

The *validity* of the age standardisation is improved if there is good correlation between pupils' test scores and age. Additionally, the test itself must have high reliability (see above) so that the results would be replicated by repeated administrations of the test.

For tests targeting a particular age range, we use a standardisation method based on *percentile norms*, the fundamental principle being that scores at the same percentile rank are comparable. Hence a student at, say, the 30th percentile in his/her age group has the same relative ability as a student at the 30th percentile in any other age group. Standardised scores would be expected to rise with students' ages, the older students tending to score more highly until they reach a plateau. The standardisation procedure that we have used for these tests is called the *non-parallel linear regression model*.[1]

---

[1] Our basic methodology follows D. G. Lewis (see *Statistical Methods in Education*, University of London Press, 1972, pp.86–96), with enhancements outlined by I. Schagen (see 'A Method for the Age Standardisation of Test Scores', *Applied Psychological Measurement*, 14, 4, December 1990, pp.387–93) and Kiek, L. A. (*ESITEMS User Guide – Age Standardisation*, Cambridge University Local Examinations Syndicate, Research and Evaluation Division, 1997, p.61.)

Analysis of the data indicates that there is a strong correlation between pupils' performances and their age, indicating that the standardised scores give a valid comparison for teachers to use to measure an individual student's relative performance, and giving a further indication of the reliability of the tests:

Correlation (Pearson's r) of test total raw score on Form A with age in months = 0.713

Correlation (Pearson's r) of test total raw score on Form B with age in months = 0.633

The slightly lower correlation for Form B suggests that some students may not have completed Form B as carefully as Form A, possibly because some did the two tests one after another. Bearing this in mind, the data supplied in this manual uses that gained from Form A, as both forms are highly correlated (see the close agreement of the overall facilities for each year): either Form is appropriate, but Form A is likely to have marginally more reliable statistics.

Table A: Standardised scores (Forms A & B)

Age in years and completed months

Raw score	7:0	7:1	7:2	7:3	7:4	7:5	7:6	7:7	7:8	7:9	7:10	7:11	8:0	8:1	8:2	8:3	Raw score
1	72	71	71	70													1
2	74	74	73	72	72	71	70										2
3	77	76	75	75	74	73	73	72	71	71	70						3
4	78	78	77	77	76	76	75	74	74	73	72	72	71	70			4
5	80	79	79	78	78	78	77	77	76	75	75	74	73	73	72	71	5
6	81	81	80	80	80	79	79	78	78	77	77	76	76	75	74	74	6
7	83	82	82	81	81	81	80	80	79	79	78	78	77	77	77	76	7
8	84	84	83	83	82	82	82	81	81	80	80	79	79	79	78	78	8
9	85	85	85	84	84	83	83	83	82	82	81	81	81	80	80	79	9
10	87	87	86	86	85	85	84	84	84	83	83	82	82	81	81	81	10
11	89	88	88	87	87	86	86	85	85	84	84	84	83	83	82	82	11
12	90	90	89	89	88	88	87	87	86	86	86	85	85	84	84	83	12
13	91	91	91	90	90	89	89	88	88	88	87	87	86	86	85	85	13
14	93	92	92	92	91	91	90	90	90	89	89	88	88	87	87	86	14
15	94	94	93	93	93	92	92	91	91	91	90	90	89	89	88	88	15
16	96	95	95	94	94	94	93	93	92	92	92	91	91	90	90	90	16
17	97	97	96	96	95	95	95	94	94	94	93	93	92	92	91	91	17
18	98	98	98	97	97	96	96	96	95	95	95	94	94	93	93	93	18
19	100	99	99	99	98	98	97	97	97	96	96	96	95	95	94	94	19
20	101	101	100	100	99	99	99	98	98	98	97	97	97	96	96	95	20
21	102	102	101	101	101	100	100	100	99	99	99	98	98	98	97	97	21
22	103	103	103	102	102	102	101	101	101	100	100	100	99	99	99	98	22
23	105	104	104	104	103	103	103	102	102	102	101	101	101	100	100	100	23
24	106	106	105	105	105	104	104	104	103	103	103	102	102	102	101	101	24
25	107	107	107	106	106	106	105	105	105	104	104	104	103	103	103	102	25
26	109	108	108	108	107	107	107	106	106	106	105	105	105	104	104	104	26
27	110	110	109	109	109	108	108	108	108	107	107	107	106	106	106	105	27
28	112	111	111	111	110	110	110	109	109	109	108	108	108	107	107	107	28
29	113	113	112	112	112	111	111	111	110	110	110	109	109	109	108	108	29
30	115	114	114	114	113	113	113	112	112	112	111	111	111	110	110	110	30
31	116	116	116	115	115	115	114	114	114	113	113	113	112	112	111	111	31
32	118	118	117	117	117	116	116	116	115	115	114	114	114	113	113	113	32
33	120	119	119	119	118	118	118	117	117	117	116	116	116	115	115	114	33
34	122	121	121	121	120	120	120	119	119	118	118	118	117	117	117	116	34
35	123	123	123	122	122	122	121	121	121	120	120	120	119	119	119	118	35
36	125	125	125	124	124	124	123	123	123	122	122	121	121	121	120	120	36
37	127	127	126	126	126	125	125	125	124	124	124	123	123	123	122	122	37
38	129	129	128	128	128	127	127	127	126	126	126	125	125	125	124	124	38
39				130	130	129	129	129	128	128	128	127	127	127	126	126	39
40											130	129	129	129	128	128	40
41																	41
42																	42
43																	43
44																	44
45																	45
46																	46
47																	47
48																	48
49																	49
50+																	50+
	7:0	7:1	7:2	7:3	7:4	7:5	7:6	7:7	7:8	7:9	7:10	7:11	8:0	8:1	8:2	8:3	

Table A: Standardised scores (Forms A & B) *cont.*

Age in years and completed months

Raw score	8:4	8:5	8:6	8:7	8:8	8:9	8:10	8:11	9:0	9:1	9:2	9:3	9:4	9:5	9:6	9:7	Raw score
1																	1
2																	2
3																	3
4																	4
5	71	70															5
6	73	72	72	71	70												6
7	75	75	74	73	73	72	71	71	70								7
8	77	77	76	75	75	74	74	73	72	72	71	71					8
9	79	78	78	77	77	76	76	75	74	74	73	73	72	71	71	70	9
10	80	80	79	79	78	78	78	77	77	76	75	75	74	74	73	72	10
11	82	81	81	80	80	80	79	79	78	78	77	77	76	76	75	74	11
12	83	83	82	82	81	81	81	80	80	79	79	78	78	77	77	77	12
13	84	84	84	83	83	82	82	82	81	81	80	80	79	79	79	78	13
14	86	85	85	85	84	84	83	83	83	82	82	81	81	80	80	80	14
15	88	87	87	86	86	85	85	84	84	83	83	83	82	82	81	81	15
16	89	89	88	88	87	87	86	86	85	85	84	84	84	83	83	82	16
17	91	90	90	89	89	88	88	87	87	86	86	86	85	85	84	84	17
18	92	92	91	91	90	90	90	89	89	88	88	87	87	86	86	85	18
19	94	93	93	92	92	91	91	91	90	90	89	89	88	88	87	87	19
20	95	95	94	94	93	93	93	92	92	91	91	90	90	90	89	89	20
21	96	96	96	95	95	94	94	94	93	93	92	92	92	91	91	90	21
22	98	97	97	97	96	96	96	95	95	94	94	93	93	93	92	92	22
23	99	99	99	98	98	97	97	97	96	96	95	95	95	94	94	93	23
24	101	100	100	100	99	99	98	98	98	97	97	96	96	96	95	95	24
25	102	102	101	101	101	100	100	99	99	99	98	98	98	97	97	96	25
26	103	103	103	102	102	102	101	101	101	100	100	99	99	99	98	98	26
27	105	105	104	104	103	103	103	102	102	102	101	101	101	100	100	99	27
28	106	106	106	105	105	105	104	104	103	103	103	102	102	102	101	101	28
29	108	107	107	107	106	106	106	105	105	105	104	104	103	103	103	102	29
30	109	109	109	108	108	107	107	107	106	106	106	105	105	105	104	104	30
31	111	110	110	110	109	109	109	108	108	108	107	107	107	106	106	105	31
32	112	112	112	111	111	111	110	110	109	109	109	108	108	108	107	107	32
33	114	114	113	113	113	112	112	112	111	111	110	110	110	109	109	109	33
34	116	115	115	115	114	114	114	113	113	113	112	112	111	111	111	110	34
35	118	117	117	117	116	116	115	115	115	114	114	114	113	113	112	112	35
36	120	119	119	119	118	118	117	117	117	116	116	115	115	115	114	114	36
37	122	121	121	121	120	120	119	119	119	118	118	117	117	117	116	116	37
38	124	123	123	123	122	122	121	121	121	120	120	120	119	119	118	118	38
39	126	125	125	125	124	124	124	123	123	122	122	122	121	121	120	120	39
40	128	127	127	127	126	126	126	125	125	125	124	124	123	123	123	122	40
41	130	130	129	129	129	128	128	128	127	127	126	126	126	125	125	124	41
42								130	129	129	129	128	128	128	127	127	42
43														130	130	129	43
44																	44
45																	45
46																	46
47																	47
48																	48
49																	49
50+																	50+
	8:4	8:5	8:6	8:7	8:8	8:9	8:10	8:11	9:0	9:1	9:2	9:3	9:4	9:5	9:6	9:7	

Table A: Standardised scores (Forms A & B) *cont.*

Age in years and completed months

Raw score	9:8	9:9	9:10	9:11	10:0	10:1	10:2	10:3	10:4	10:5	10:6	10:7	10:8	10:9	Raw score
1															1
2															2
3															3
4															4
5															5
6															6
7															7
8															8
9															9
10	72	71	71												10
11	74	73	73	72	71	71	70								11
12	76	75	75	74	73	73	72	72	71	71					12
13	78	77	77	76	76	75	74	74	73	73	72	71	71	70	13
14	79	79	78	78	77	77	76	76	75	75	74	73	73	72	14
15	81	80	80	79	79	78	78	78	77	77	76	75	75	74	15
16	82	82	81	81	80	80	80	79	79	78	78	77	77	76	16
17	83	83	83	82	82	81	81	81	80	80	79	79	78	78	17
18	85	84	84	84	83	83	82	82	82	81	81	80	80	79	18
19	86	86	85	85	85	84	84	83	83	82	82	82	81	81	19
20	88	88	87	87	86	86	85	85	84	84	83	83	83	82	20
21	90	89	89	88	88	87	87	86	86	85	85	84	84	84	21
22	91	91	90	90	89	89	89	88	88	87	87	86	86	85	22
23	93	92	92	92	91	91	90	90	89	89	88	88	87	87	23
24	94	94	94	93	93	92	92	91	91	90	90	89	89	88	24
25	96	96	95	95	94	94	93	93	92	92	92	91	91	90	25
26	97	97	97	96	96	95	95	94	94	94	93	93	92	92	26
27	99	99	98	98	97	97	96	96	96	95	95	94	94	93	27
28	100	100	100	99	99	98	98	98	97	97	96	96	95	95	28
29	102	102	101	101	100	100	100	99	99	98	98	97	97	97	29
30	103	103	103	102	102	102	101	101	100	100	100	99	99	98	30
31	105	105	104	104	103	103	103	102	102	102	101	101	100	100	31
32	107	106	106	105	105	105	104	104	104	103	103	102	102	101	32
33	108	108	107	107	107	106	106	105	105	105	104	104	104	103	33
34	110	109	109	109	108	108	108	107	107	106	106	106	105	105	34
35	112	111	111	110	110	110	109	109	108	108	108	107	107	106	35
36	113	113	113	112	112	111	111	111	110	110	109	109	109	108	36
37	115	115	115	114	114	113	113	113	112	112	111	111	110	110	37
38	117	117	117	116	116	115	115	114	114	114	113	113	112	112	38
39	120	119	119	118	118	118	117	117	116	116	115	115	114	114	39
40	122	121	121	121	120	120	119	119	118	118	118	117	117	116	40
41	124	124	123	123	122	122	122	121	121	120	120	119	119	119	41
42	126	126	126	125	125	124	124	124	123	123	122	122	121	121	42
43	129	128	128	128	127	127	126	126	126	125	125	124	124	123	43
44					130	129	129	129	128	128	127	127	126	126	44
45											130	129	129	129	45
46															46
47															47
48															48
49															49
50+															50+
	9:8	9:9	9:10	9:11	10:0	10:1	10:2	10:3	10:4	10:5	10:6	10:7	10:8	10:9	

Table A: Standardised scores (Forms A & B) *cont*

Age in years and completed months

Raw score	10:10	10:11	11:0	11:1	11:2	11:3	11:4	11:5	11:6	11:7	11:8	11:9	11:10	11:11	Raw score
1															1
2															2
3															3
4															4
5															5
6															6
7															7
8															8
9															9
10															10
11															11
12															12
13															13
14	72	71	71												14
15	74	73	73	72	71	71	70								15
16	76	75	75	74	73	73	72	72	71	71					16
17	77	77	77	76	75	75	74	74	73	73	72	71	71	70	17
18	79	78	78	78	77	77	76	76	75	74	74	73	73	72	18
19	80	80	80	79	79	78	78	77	77	76	76	75	75	74	19
20	82	81	81	81	80	80	79	79	78	78	78	77	77	76	20
21	83	83	82	82	82	81	81	80	80	79	79	79	78	78	21
22	85	84	84	83	83	83	82	82	81	81	80	80	80	79	22
23	86	86	85	85	84	84	84	83	83	82	82	81	81	81	23
24	88	87	87	86	86	85	85	85	84	84	83	83	82	82	24
25	90	89	89	88	88	87	87	86	86	85	85	84	84	83	25
26	91	91	90	90	89	89	88	88	87	87	86	86	85	85	26
27	93	92	92	92	91	91	90	90	89	89	88	88	87	87	27
28	95	94	94	93	93	92	92	91	91	90	90	89	89	88	28
29	96	96	95	95	94	94	93	93	93	92	92	91	91	90	29
30	98	97	97	96	96	96	95	95	94	94	93	93	92	92	30
31	99	99	99	98	98	97	97	96	96	95	95	94	94	94	31
32	101	101	100	100	99	99	98	98	98	97	97	96	96	95	32
33	103	102	102	101	101	101	100	100	99	99	98	98	97	97	33
34	104	104	104	103	103	102	102	101	101	101	100	100	99	99	34
35	106	106	105	105	104	104	104	103	103	102	102	101	101	100	35
36	108	107	107	107	106	106	105	105	104	104	104	103	103	102	36
37	110	109	109	108	108	107	107	107	106	106	105	105	104	104	37
38	111	111	111	110	110	109	109	108	108	108	107	107	106	106	38
39	114	113	113	112	112	111	111	110	110	109	109	109	108	108	39
40	116	115	115	114	114	113	113	113	112	112	111	111	110	110	40
41	118	118	117	117	116	116	115	115	114	114	113	113	112	112	41
42	120	120	120	119	119	118	118	117	117	116	116	115	115	114	42
43	123	123	122	122	121	121	120	120	119	119	118	118	117	117	43
44	126	125	125	124	124	123	123	122	122	121	121	120	120	119	44
45	128	128	127	127	126	126	126	125	125	124	124	123	123	122	45
46				130	129	129	128	128	127	127	126	126	125	125	46
47										130	129	129	128	128	47
48															48
49															49
50+															50+
	10:10	10:11	11:0	11:1	11:2	11:3	11:4	11:5	11:6	11:7	11:8	11:9	11:10	11:11	

Table A: Standardised scores (Forms A & B) *cont*

Age in years and completed months

Raw score	12:0 12:2	12:3 12:5	12:6 12:8	12:9 12:11	13:0 13:2	13:3 13:5	13:6 13:8	13:9 13:11	14:0 14:2	14:3 14:5	14:6 14:8	14:9 14:11	15:0 15:2	15:3 15:5	15:6 15:8	15:9 15:11	Raw score
10																	10
11																	11
12																	12
13																	13
14																	14
15																	15
16																	16
17																	17
18	71																18
19	73	71															19
20	75	73	72	70													20
21	77	75	74	72	70												21
22	78	77	75	74	72	71											22
23	80	78	77	76	74	72	71										23
24	81	80	79	77	76	74	73	71									24
25	83	81	80	79	78	76	75	73	71								25
26	84	83	82	80	79	78	76	75	73	72	70						26
27	86	84	83	82	80	79	78	77	75	73	72	70					27
28	87	86	84	83	82	81	79	78	77	75	74	72	71				28
29	89	88	86	85	83	82	81	79	78	77	75	74	72	71			29
30	91	89	88	86	85	83	82	81	80	78	77	76	74	73	71		30
31	93	91	90	88	86	85	84	82	81	80	79	77	76	74	73	71	31
32	94	93	91	90	88	87	85	84	82	81	80	79	77	76	75	73	32
33	96	95	93	92	90	89	87	85	84	83	81	80	79	78	76	75	33
34	98	96	95	93	92	90	89	87	85	84	83	82	80	79	78	76	34
35	100	98	97	95	94	92	91	89	87	86	84	83	82	80	79	78	35
36	101	100	98	97	96	94	92	91	89	88	86	84	83	82	81	79	36
37	103	102	100	99	97	96	94	93	91	90	88	86	85	83	82	81	37
38	105	104	102	101	99	98	96	95	93	91	90	88	86	85	83	82	38
39	107	105	104	103	101	100	98	97	95	93	92	90	88	87	85	84	39
40	109	107	106	105	103	102	100	99	97	95	94	92	90	89	87	85	40
41	111	109	108	107	105	104	102	101	99	97	96	94	92	91	89	87	41
42	113	112	110	109	107	106	104	103	101	99	98	96	94	93	91	89	42
43	116	114	113	111	109	108	106	105	103	101	100	98	96	95	93	91	43
44	118	117	115	113	112	110	109	107	105	104	102	100	99	97	95	93	44
45	121	119	118	116	114	113	111	109	108	106	104	103	101	99	97	95	45
46	124	122	121	119	117	115	114	112	110	108	107	105	103	101	99	98	46
47	127	125	124	122	120	119	117	115	113	111	109	107	106	104	102	100	47
48		129	127	125	124	122	120	118	116	114	112	110	108	106	104	102	48
49				129	127	125	123	122	119	117	115	113	111	109	107	105	49
50						129	127	125	123	121	119	117	114	112	110	108	50
51								129	127	125	123	121	118	116	114	111	51
52										129	127	125	123	120	118	115	52
53												130	127	125	122	120	53
54															128	125	54
55																	55
56																	56
57																	57
58																	58
59																	59
60																	60
	12:0 12:2	12:3 12:5	12:6 12:8	12:9 12:11	13:0 13:2	13:3 13:5	13:6 13:8	13:9 13:11	14:0 14:2	14:3 14:5	14:6 14:8	14:9 14:11	15:0 15:2	15:3 15:5	15:6 15:8	15:9 15:11	

Table A: Standardised scores (Forms A & B) *cont*

Age in years and completed months

Raw score	16:0 16:2	16:3 16:5	16:6 16:8	16:9 16:11	17:0 17:2	17:3 17:5	17:6 17:8	17:9 17:11	18:0 18:2	18:3 18:5	18:6 18:8	18:9 18:11	19:0 19:2	19:3 19:5	19:6 19:8	19:9 19:11	20:0+	Raw score
10																		10
11																		11
12																		12
13																		13
14																		14
15																		15
16																		16
17																		17
18																		18
19																		19
20																		20
21																		21
22																		22
23																		23
24																		24
25																		25
26																		26
27																		27
28																		28
29																		29
30																		30
31																		31
32	72	70																32
33	73	72	71															33
34	75	74	72	71														34
35	77	75	74	72	71													35
36	78	77	75	74	73	71												36
37	79	78	77	76	74	73	71	70										37
38	81	80	78	77	76	74	73	72	70									38
39	82	81	80	79	77	76	75	73	72	71								39
40	84	83	81	80	79	77	76	75	73	72	71							40
41	85	84	83	81	80	79	78	76	75	74	72	71						41
42	87	86	84	83	82	80	79	78	77	75	74	73	71					42
43	89	88	86	84	83	82	80	79	78	77	75	74	73	71	70			43
44	91	90	88	86	85	83	82	81	79	78	77	76	74	73	72	70		44
45	94	92	90	88	86	85	83	82	81	79	78	77	76	74	73	72	71	45
46	96	94	92	90	88	87	85	84	82	81	80	78	77	76	75	73	73	46
47	98	96	94	92	91	89	87	85	84	82	81	80	79	77	76	75	74	47
48	100	99	97	95	93	91	89	87	85	84	83	81	80	79	78	76	75	48
49	103	101	99	97	95	93	91	89	87	86	84	83	81	80	79	78	77	49
50	106	104	102	100	98	95	94	92	90	88	86	84	83	82	80	79	78	50
51	109	107	104	102	100	98	96	94	92	90	88	86	84	83	82	80	80	51
52	112	110	108	105	103	101	99	96	94	92	90	88	86	85	83	82	81	52
53	117	114	111	109	106	104	102	99	97	95	93	91	89	87	85	83	83	53
54	122	119	116	113	110	107	105	102	100	98	95	93	91	89	87	85	84	54
55	128	125	121	118	115	111	108	106	103	100	98	96	93	91	89	87	86	55
56			128	124	121	117	113	110	107	104	101	99	96	94	92	89	88	56
57					128	124	120	115	112	108	105	102	99	97	94	92	91	57
58							128	123	119	114	110	106	103	100	97	95	93	58
59									129	123	117	112	108	104	101	98	96	59
60												122+	115+	110+	105+	102+	100+	60
	16:0 16:2	16:3 16:5	16:6 16:8	16:9 16:11	17:0 17:2	17:3 17:5	17:6 17:8	17:9 17:11	18:0 18:2	18:3 18:5	18:6 18:8	18:9 18:11	19:0 19:2	19:3 19:5	19:6 19:8	19:9 19:11	20:0+	

Table B: Facilities for questions for each year cohort

Form A facilities for questions for each year cohort, expressed as decimals

Question number	Year 3 sample (286)	Year 4 sample (303)	Year 5 sample (275)	Year 6 sample (220)	Year 7 sample (945)	Year 8 sample (537)	Year 9 sample (442)	Year 10 sample (424)	Year 11 sample (313)	Year 12 sample (157)	Year 13 sample (128)	Trainee sample (62)
A1	.59	.69	.84	.81	.91	.91	.93	.92	.96	.97	.95	.98
A2	.54	.66	.73	.74	.83	.81	.92	.91	.93	.97	.95	.98
A3	.66	.79	.88	.87	.94	.96	.97	.98	.98	.99	.98	.97
A4	.25	.27	.37	.42	.58	.69	.72	.78	.83	.90	.85	.90
A5	.61	.72	.84	.88	.92	.94	.95	.96	.96	.97	.97	.97
A6	.58	.71	.77	.86	.90	.91	.95	.94	.96	.98	.97	.97
A7	.57	.72	.83	.90	.93	.93	.96	.97	.98	.97	.98	.98
A8	.57	.76	.89	.93	.94	.96	.97	.98	.96	.99	.99	.98
A9	.72	.85	.92	.91	.97	.96	.98	.98	.99	.97	.99	.92
A10	.30	.51	.69	.81	.92	.91	.95	.96	.96	.97	.98	.95
A11	.58	.79	.88	.91	.96	.95	.97	.98	.98	.97	.98	.95
A12	.54	.72	.82	.87	.92	.93	.95	.96	.96	.96	.99	.98
A13	.24	.38	.56	.74	.84	.88	.92	.94	.93	.97	.98	.95
A14	.40	.64	.75	.77	.83	.86	.87	.92	.95	.93	.95	.87
A15	.42	.62	.74	.79	.86	.89	.91	.92	.93	.95	.96	.89
A16	.41	.71	.83	.87	.93	.93	.95	.96	.97	.97	.98	.90
A17	.37	.62	.72	.79	.88	.91	.93	.93	.96	.97	.95	.87
A18	.33	.46	.56	.52	.69	.71	.74	.78	.79	.79	.83	.69
A19	.15	.24	.31	.35	.34	.37	.38	.44	.38	.59	.47	.40
A20	.47	.70	.75	.77	.75	.70	.73	.77	.78	.80	.81	.73
A21	.32	.48	.61	.65	.75	.79	.81	.83	.85	.91	.91	.89
A22	.44	.60	.66	.85	.92	.93	.93	.97	.97	.97	.97	.97
A23	.22	.27	.32	.46	.62	.67	.73	.80	.81	.89	.93	.84
A24	.17	.31	.47	.72	.83	.85	.89	.93	.93	.99	.98	.97
A25	.28	.38	.46	.62	.81	.82	.88	.90	.91	.96	.99	.90
A26	.37	.55	.63	.80	.89	.92	.95	.96	.94	1	.98	1
A27	.36	.55	.68	.86	.91	.91	.93	.93	.94	.96	.97	.95
A28	.16	.22	.22	.37	.62	.63	.72	.78	.84	.89	.95	.90
A29	.14	.31	.34	.45	.56	.50	.53	.55	.56	.78	.76	.65
A30	.17	.26	.37	.50	.70	.74	.78	.78	.77	.84	.92	.81
A31	.15	.30	.49	.64	.84	.85	.90	.93	.94	.98	1	.98
A32	.20	.35	.45	.60	.72	.76	.81	.87	.86	.96	.98	.95
A33	.12	.30	.33	.50	.69	.74	.79	.82	.84	.96	.94	.92
A34	.13	.23	.29	.38	.41	.39	.44	.50	.50	.52	.57	.60
A35	.17	.26	.35	.33	.45	.46	.46	.49	.51	.65	.63	.68
A36	.25	.38	.56	.69	.75	.77	.77	.85	.82	.90	.91	.85
A37	.17	.27	.38	.55	.58	.63	.64	.67	.68	.66	.73	.60
A38	.18	.26	.31	.46	.56	.58	.64	.71	.73	.80	.77	.79
A39	.90	.17	.27	.46	.59	.61	.71	.75	.79	.97	.96	.84
A40	.50	.16	.31	.50	.56	.59	.67	.73	.73	.95	.88	.76
A41	.30	.10	.16	.26	.36	.41	.49	.57	.68	.83	.85	.69
A42	.30	.14	.20	.31	.40	.45	.48	.55	.63	.80	.77	.55
A43	.60	.14	.27	.45	.55	.61	.70	.71	.74	.87	.88	.87
A44	.60	.14	.19	.39	.46	.55	.58	.68	.67	.87	.84	.73
A45	.60	.70	.90	.19	.30	.40	.52	.63	.68	.88	.88	.76
A46	.14	.16	.28	.30	.33	.37	.44	.50	.50	.78	.73	.65
A47	.11	.12	.24	.29	.34	.38	.45	.51	.58	.82	.73	.63
A48	.90	.13	.19	.34	.39	.46	.44	.45	.48	.66	.63	.55
A49	.70	.12	.27	.45	.55	.61	.70	.81	.79	.94	.94	.95
A50	.90	.70	.80	.18	.22	.25	.33	.34	.46	.69	.70	.58
A51	.80	.12	.15	.29	.31	.31	.46	.54	.53	.73	.76	.71
A52	.10	.24	.28	.58	.61	.61	.70	.74	.72	.90	.90	.87
A53	.50	.11	.16	.25	.36	.36	.48	.47	.57	.73	.73	.66
A54	.10	.18	.37	.55	.60	.55	.64	.69	.71	.83	.86	.81
A55	.70	.12	.17	.27	.37	.36	.45	.49	.59	.80	.82	.74
A56	.90	.30	.30	.80	.60	.70	.70	.90	.70	.15	.18	.60
A57	.10	.19	.28	.42	.43	.40	.43	.43	.52	.64	.60	.61
A58	.12	.16	.29	.50	.59	.69	.69	.78	.79	.93	.93	.92
A59	.70	.13	.17	.38	.49	.50	.61	.64	.65	.84	.78	.73
A60	.80	.11	.15	.25	.30	.40	.52	.54	.61	.81	.77	.79
Average Total score	14.8	21.4	26.8	33.2	38.3	39.7	42.7	44.8	46	51.6	51.5	48.5

Form B facilities for questions for each year cohort, expressed as decimals

Question number	Year 3 sample (286)	Year 4 sample (303)	Year 5 sample (275)	Year 6 sample (220)	Year 7 sample (945)	Year 8 sample (537)	Year 9 sample (442)	Year 10 sample (424)	Year 11 sample (313)	Year 12 sample (157)	Year 13 sample (128)	Trainee sample (62)
B1	.52	.75	.85	.91	.93	.93	.94	.95	.96	.97	.98	.97
B2	.70	.83	.91	.96	.97	.98	.98	.98	.99	.99	.98	1
B3	.72	.87	.92	.95	.97	.97	.98	.98	.98	.98	.98	1
B4	.49	.64	.75	.85	.81	.84	.86	.87	.88	.91	.95	.92
B5	.41	.60	.72	.74	.82	.84	.85	.92	.90	.96	.95	.92
B6	.60	.77	.85	.86	.93	.93	.94	.94	.94	.94	.91	.95
B7	.53	.69	.83	.84	.91	.93	.90	.93	.93	.95	.96	.87
B8	.54	.69	.76	.76	.77	.80	.79	.85	.84	.89	.88	.92
B9	.66	.73	.83	.88	.92	.91	.93	.95	.93	.98	.95	.92
B10	.65	.83	.86	.94	.95	.96	.97	.96	.96	.97	.98	.97
B11	.23	.29	.46	.53	.62	.74	.80	.81	.84	.93	.96	.90
B12	.28	.51	.76	.76	.91	.89	.94	.94	.92	.97	.96	.98
B13	.38	.65	.67	.76	.80	.88	.87	.89	.90	.98	.88	.87
B14	.25	.39	.52	.55	.64	.70	.74	.80	.81	.92	.84	.87
B15	.23	.40	.58	.62	.74	.78	.80	.85	.87	.94	.97	.92
B16	.20	.34	.52	.53	.66	.73	.75	.81	.81	.96	.91	.89
B17	.22	.38	.51	.60	.71	.77	.83	.84	.85	.99	.90	.94
B18	.18	.14	.23	.23	.39	.35	.33	.36	.38	.53	.46	.29
B19	.41	.56	.61	.70	.76	.79	.84	.83	.81	.94	.87	.94
B20	.51	.62	.65	.72	.77	.77	.74	.73	.74	.75	.77	.71
B21	.36	.44	.49	.40	.47	.47	.40	.50	.48	.55	.54	.55
B22	.26	.45	.45	.60	.65	.63	.72	.76	.73	.90	.87	.87
B23	.17	.18	.20	.23	.34	.39	.43	.56	.68	.82	.82	.65
B24	.35	.57	.65	.81	.89	.88	.91	.95	.91	.96	.97	.92
B25	.17	.32	.48	.66	.81	.78	.81	.82	.82	.91	.91	.84
B26	.13	.16	.20	.36	.55	.67	.80	.85	.91	.97	.97	.92
B27	.67	.79	.79	.89	.92	.92	.94	.96	.92	.97	.95	.95
B28	.40	.49	.43	.50	.53	.58	.56	.63	.56	.68	.72	.58
B29	.12	.15	.18	.21	.34	.36	.45	.48	.45	.67	.71	.55
B30	.80	.12	.11	.11	.10	.12	.11	.16	.20	.34	.24	.29
B31	.18	.27	.33	.38	.40	.41	.37	.37	.40	.36	.36	.52
B32	.17	.29	.34	.47	.69	.71	.74	.76	.81	.87	.91	.82
B33	.28	.38	.44	.56	.51	.49	.57	.62	.58	.71	.68	.69
B34	.30	.48	.53	.64	.70	.66	.67	.66	.69	.66	.66	.73
B35	.19	.29	.28	.29	.30	.31	.30	.35	.32	.50	.52	.40
B36	.27	.38	.47	.65	.73	.76	.79	.80	.79	.94	.89	.94
B37	.19	.31	.32	.39	.43	.44	.49	.52	.56	.65	.73	.66
B38	.16	.37	.44	.58	.71	.70	.79	.83	.82	.94	.92	.94
B39	.19	.38	.47	.68	.66	.62	.69	.71	.70	.85	.84	.79
B40	.12	.27	.34	.61	.62	.57	.62	.65	.64	.83	.83	.79
B41	.90	.24	.35	.55	.59	.59	.67	.69	.69	.87	.90	.89
B42	.60	.22	.25	.48	.53	.52	.57	.64	.59	.78	.80	.76
B43	.60	.17	.28	.44	.54	.55	.61	.64	.66	.87	.87	.77
B44	.80	.19	.27	.54	.52	.57	.62	.68	.64	.76	.84	.79
B45	.90	.25	.36	.52	.66	.65	.76	.81	.80	.98	.92	.90
B46	.80	.20	.27	.46	.54	.50	.64	.68	.69	.88	.83	.77
B47	.13	.18	.15	.34	.34	.45	.51	.59	.55	.76	.80	.79
B48	.13	.20	.21	.29	.31	.34	.44	.47	.52	.64	.65	.53
B49	.16	.20	.21	.31	.40	.39	.53	.56	.57	.73	.75	.66
B50	.30	.70	.13	.17	.25	.34	.37	.51	.58	.68	.73	.71
B51	.80	.21	.33	.55	.58	.61	.65	.70	.71	.78	.81	.73
B52	.70	.12	.23	.40	.56	.61	.67	.77	.78	.94	.88	.90
B53	.20	.60	.80	.19	.29	.37	.41	.58	.60	.77	.77	.71
B54	.60	.80	.13	.13	.11	.12	.14	.23	.23	.41	.32	.29
B55	.60	.21	.40	.64	.69	.74	.72	.82	.82	.90	.88	.84
B56	.11	.17	.32	.54	.67	.76	.76	.88	.88	.96	.95	.94
B57	.70	.90	.16	.36	.46	.53	.64	.64	.72	.89	.88	.87
B58	.12	.29	.43	.67	.74	.66	.79	.83	.83	.97	.92	.95
B59	.70	.13	.35	.60	.70	.77	.79	.86	.87	.95	.95	.90
B60	.70	.60	.11	.20	.36	.30	.31	.37	.50	.68	.74	.48
Average total score	15.4	22.5	27.2	33.5	37.5	38.6	40.7	43.2	43.5	49.8	49.3	47.4